• Masi

BANGLADESH
Dacca • • Baidya Bazar

Kuala Lumpur • MALAYSIA • Bario

Foreword

The earth is a home we all share, each with our own special corner. That corner – whether city, mountain, or frozen Arctic – affects the way we grow and the things we use. None of us choose where we're born, but we quickly accept it as home.

People who live in corners other than our own often seem far away and sometimes a bit peculiar. It's easy, whether we live in Peru or Britain, to think of others as different. Even television, while it brings distant people into our homes, can still keep us worlds apart.

Many of us have fixed ideas of what other people are like – all British men wear bowler hats; all desert people ride camels; all jungle people swing on vines like Tarzan. It was a special chance, therefore, that I could travel to different parts of the world while making the Yorkshire Television series **Two-Way Ticket**. I stayed with six children and their families in six very different corners of the earth.

But travellers are not the best source of information about other parts of the world, and that's why I asked the children to describe their lives for themselves. In turn, they came to Britain to record the programmes and to stay with my family. Only Fatimettou was unable to come because of family objections. England seemed too far away and too foreign.

This book tries to look at our world not from the outside but from within.

Sarah Hobson

First published 1982 by
Macdonald & Co
(Publishers) Ltd
Maxwell House
Worship Street
London EC2A 2EN

© Sarah Hobson 1982

ISBN 0 356 07863 9

Printed and bound by
Purnell & Sons
(Book Production) Ltd
Paulton, England

Editor Annabel McLaren
Designer Carole Ash
Production John Moulder
Artwork Rudolph Britto

TWO-WAY TICKET

Sarah Hobson

Photographs by Alan Harbour

Macdonald

Preface

Three years ago Macdonald Educational published, in collaboration with UNICEF, a book about children called *My World* as a special contribution towards the International Year of the Child. Like that book, *Two-Way Ticket* is about children in different parts of the world, living different lives in different surroundings, but with the same needs and hopes and the same global future.

The United Nations has now given UNICEF, the UN Children's Fund, the main responsibility for children throughout the world. Its member governments work together to share resources in such a way that children in the so-called 'developing' countries can, wherever possible, have the same opportunities as those in 'industrialised' countries to satisfy their hunger, wear enough clothing to keep them warm, have a roof over their heads, go to school and to a health centre when they are sick.

So UNICEF encourages governments and local groups to protect children such as those in this book, to give them a chance to grow up happily and in good health, able to make their own contribution to life around them and to world society. Sometimes this is done by providing seeds and tools for school gardens, or by providing pumps to bring clean water to villages. Paper may be provided for school textbooks, special food supplements may be given to hungry babies whose mothers cannot afford to feed them properly, and training may be given to a village health worker who can help families to take good care of their children.

All children need food, love and protection, and to know more about each other so that they will understand the need to work together for a better, fairer world. UNICEF thanks Sarah Hobson for this book, and Macdonald for publishing it. We know you will enjoy reading it.

James Grant
UNICEF Executive Director

Sarah Hobson has produced, for UNICEF, Development Education slide packs on three of the regions featured in *Two-Way Ticket*. They are on Mauritania, Peru and Malaysia and are available from the UK Committee for UNICEF, 46-48 Osnaburgh St., London NW1 3PU.

Contents

Mountains
Oscar Galindo

He loved the broad spaces and the magnificent grandeur of the Andes...he attributed to the mountains all the shapes and characters imaginable, and he spent long hours watching them.

from a book by the Peruvian writer Ciro Alegria

Mountains exert such a strong fascination that some people risk their lives to conquer a peak. Last year, in the Alps, more than 200 people were killed while mountaineering. But many climbers claim that as they reach the peaks they can feel the closeness of God.

In every continent, people believe that mountains are holy. Thousands of people make long and often difficult pilgrimages up them.

Mountains provide not only spiritual satisfaction but material resources as well – timber for houses, electricity from mountain dams, minerals and precious stones. These are often extracted for use in other parts of the world with little consideration for the needs of the local community. One mineral in particular – gold – has always lured people to mountains.

450 years ago, the prospect of gold attracted a band of Spanish soldiers, known as the *Conquistadores,* to the Andes of South America. They smashed the mountain civilisation of the Incas and declared themselves the new rulers. They seized vast quantities of gold objects, and slaughtered thousands of mountain Indians. Indians were forced to work in mines to extract gold and silver which was shipped back to Spain by the ton.

Out of twelve million Indians, nearly ten million died. Of those that remained, many fled into the remotest parts of the mountains for safety. Today, the descendants of such survivors still live in small communitities high in the Andes, particularly in Ecuador, Bolivia and Peru.

One of them, Cuchoquesera in Peru, is the home of Oscar Galindo. It lies at a height of 3,800 metres – two miles above sea level.

Life on the land

The land around Cuchoquesera was first documented by the Spanish in 1595. But they did not seize it from the Indians as in other parts of the Andes – probably because it is so remote and unproductive.

'There are winds that come from the highlands that make the climate very cold,' says Oscar. 'It can even damage your health. At night, with no sun, there is frost and ice like winter.'

Because of the height and intense climate his family can grow only a few crops, such as potatoes and barley. They eat what they grow. For breakfast, Oscar has soup made from beans and barley. He often misses lunch since he is far away from the house. At night he has more soup, potatoes and sometimes mutton.

Each morning Oscar gets up at four to help with the work. His father wants to see things improve. He has planted eucalyptus trees, grown better pasture,

'My father grows oats for the animals. He does things properly. I respect him very much. He's one of the community leaders and he's always trying to help people who are poorer than him.'

'This is the leader of the community sounding the trumpet for the people of Cuchoquesera to come. We are cleaning the channel that brings water down to the community. We do it whenever there's a shortage of water in summer. If anyone doesn't turn up, the leaders make them pay a fine or give up one of their animals. People work together for about eight days every month.'

10

'We spin and weave our own wool. We make all our own clothes – trousers, skirts, ponchos and all sorts of belts.'

'When I was eight years old, my mother gave me a sheep. Only one, but then I increased the number because lambs were born. Now I have ten of my own. I mix mine with the rest of the flock. In the holidays I'm the one who looks after the sheep.'

and bred stronger strains of sheep with the help of development organisations from other countries. Sometimes he walks twenty miles to help another community plant potatoes or build its own sheep dip.

Oscar loves the community of Cuchoquesera. Its seventy five families have together built a school, a church, a community hall and a shop. They each have their own plot for growing food, but they jointly own the mountain pastures that surround the community. Here families graze their own animals and take it in turns to look after a communal flock.

It takes twelve hours to walk from one end of the pastures to another. When Oscar takes the sheep to graze, he moves much more slowly. 'I always want to take them up into the hilliest parts. From there, I can see all the world, especially Cuchoquesera.'

11

Town life

Most Indian children in the Andes do not go to secondary school. This is usually because there is no school nearby and it is too expensive to go to town. The children are also needed by their parents to help with the work.

Those that do go are mainly boys. There are four from Cuchoquesera, including Oscar. They travel for five or six hours by lorry across the mountains to Ayacucho, where they stay for the term.

At first, Oscar hated school. 'Nobody treated me well,' he says. 'All the lessons were in Spanish, and I only spoke Quechua. I wasn't able to understand. Some of the schoolchildren beat me up. They didn't like me. They hated poor students, the Indians, as they called us. I suppose they thought they were better, living in towns, speaking Spanish, being richer. Without Spanish, I couldn't answer back.'

The pressures of town life are many. Some Indians try to hide their origins by wearing western clothes and never speaking Quechua. At fourteen Oscar wears school uniform, instead of his poncho and black wool trousers. But he cares too much about his parents and his community to pretend he is not Indian.

He lives with his two older brothers in a small house that was built by their father for about thirty pounds. It would cost too much to have electricity or drains. A tap in the next door house gives water for a few hours each day.

The three brothers cook, shop, clean the house and wash their own clothes. Oscar especially looks after the house. In the evenings, children from the neighbourhood often join them to play the guitar and tell stories in Quechua. Many of them are cousins, who expect to stay in town in order to find paid work.

'This is Ruben, my brother, (right) helping me with my homework. He's the clever one. Every time I have difficulties he helps me because he knows more – especially in maths. He'll probably get a good job and do well for the family. I'm not sure how well I'll do. I'd like to be a driver or a doctor, but it depends on my progress at school, and I'm finding it a bit hard.'

'My older brother gives me money to do the shopping. He earns it in the market.'

'When I'm in town I do the cooking, but my mother cooks in Cuchoquesera. I think about her a lot when I'm in town. I miss her. I also miss my father and all the family. And my sheep.'

'When I first arrived (left) I was very afraid of everything. Life in town is a mess.'

Spirits and God

When the Spanish soldiers conquered Peru, Spanish priests came to convert the Indians to Christianity. Today, the majority are Catholic, but some are evangelical. Nevertheless, old beliefs about mountain spirits remain.

'Every mountain has a name, has a spirit. My father used to make offerings to the mountain spirits. He would take fruit and flowers to a ceremonial place in the rocks. He would talk with the spirit and ask the spirit to protect his family and animals from danger and illness.'

Today, Oscar's father no longer asks the mountain spirits to help him. He feels changing methods of farming bring better results. Once he was very poor and always drunk. Now he dips the sheep himself and plants new types of barley.

For Oscar, the spirits seem very close. 'About four years ago, I was playing among some rocks. People think it's a place for bad spirits. Suddenly I fell down. I was badly shocked, and became ill – perhaps from the bad spirit. Very ill. My father was even preparing the coffin because he thought I was going to die. He called in the medicine man who treated me with herbs. Then he called an evangelical priest from Ayacucho. He came to the house and started to pray. He prayed for three weeks. Then I began to get better. The spirit went away.'

The spirits live in the mountains. 'Whenever I sleep out in the open at night, I'm scared at the thought of the evil spirits. There are also some thieves around – and foxes – that might steal our sheep. If an evil spirit approaches, a person must make a strong stand and say, "Bad spirit, go away, in the name of Jesus, go."'

There are good spirits as well and Oscar knows their places across the mountainside – a small stone which is just right as a seat, a huge outcrop of rock that gives shelter from wind and rain, a tall cairn to aim his sling at, and a clear, deep pool for swimming.

'When there is an evil spirit, I wake up and come out of the hut. The radio keeps away spirits with its noise and antenna.'

'Many families in the community are now evangelical. My father says his life has improved since he became evangelical.'

'My father is making a cross from grass and flowers to offer to the mountain spirit. He doesn't do the ceremony any more because he's become evangelical.'

'The medicine man holds flowers either side of your head and chants, "Illness, leave this body and do not touch this person." He grows his own plants for medicine. Not so many people visit him now we've got a first-aid cupboard in the community hall.'

Oscar in Britain

DAY 1

Snowed in! Oscar and Humberto the interpreter struggle through snow to get to our house. Tales of the journey from Peru. 'It was a very big plane. When I went in, I felt I was being swallowed. When the plane took off, the earth started to shake. I thought it was an earthquake. I was sweating from cold, I was so afraid. When the plane was very high up, I looked down and saw the snow below me. All my life I've looked *up* to see the snow on the mountain tops. I kept trying to see my community. I could see all the mountains, the jungles, the ocean. I didn't sleep for all the fifteen hours.' Early bed.

DAY 2

Weather terrible. Foggy, damp, dark. 'I'd be very sad if at home the sky was grey.' But a sudden clearing of the skies and soft afternoon sunshine. 'Your sun is like our dawn.' First time in snow. Too cold. Inside the house too hot. New Year party. Shocked at coldness of ice cream.

DAY 3

Oscar quietly observant. 'How can a man be allowed in the kitchen?' Later, 'Parents play with their children more here than they do at home.' Later still, 'It's good, the help the man gives here. They should do it at home but they don't. They never go into the kitchen. They've got other things to do, like working in the fields.' Favourite foods so far — soup, chips, coke, and masses of sugar in tea.

DAY 4

Football match. Leicester beat Southampton 3-1 and Keegan injured! 'There were so many people. And noise like a storm. We cheered and cheered. I did, for Keegan.'

DAY 5

TV interview. Great success. Last scene — things from Peru used in UK. Tinned sardines and pilchards. Copper wire for fridges. Lead and zinc in cars; gold in computer terminals. Nuts in chocolate. The potato and guinea pig — brought to Europe from Peru 400 years ago. Coca Cola — named from coca leaf of Peru. Used in early recipes, banned as a drug, but name stuck. Now rich Peruvians drink Coca Cola, while poor Peruvians chew coca leaf against hunger.

DAY 7

Visit home where boys sent for truancy, theft, delinquency. Many with family problems. Oscar a bit anxious when hearing they could be violent. In his community, trained 'not to lie, to steal or be lazy.' Bombarded with questions and curiosity. He is curious too. 'Why are you here, why did you do it, don't you miss your parents?' Wide-eyed that some say no. Into gym — smashed up. Boy who did it clearing up. Shows Oscar how to jump on trampoline. At end of tour, Oscar states firmly, 'I like them.' A boy comes rushing up and thrusts a note into his hand. 'Dear Oscar, if you send me some of your fishing tackle from Peru, I'll send you some of mine.'

DAY 6

Yorkshire dales and hill farm. Seemed more at home with the sheep than the farmer himself. Sheep took to him, too — especially with his poncho. Could have been Peru (see pages 4-5). Coke bottling factory a contrast. An army of bottles. Caseful given to Oscar, plus bottle fitted with radio. 'Sarah calls me Oscar Coke because I love Coke. At home, I don't have the money to buy it.'

DAY 8

Watches TV programme about African boy walking from village to big city. Total identification. 'I'm just like him. Staring in wonder. The cities so big, the buildings too high. The roads, the noise, my first train.' Longing to be back home.

DAY 9

London at a standstill. Blizzards. Train two hours late from Leeds. Oscar unmoved by collapse of plans to sight-see. Looks out for his pet joke — animals leading humans! 'It's very funny the way the man just follows. At home, the dog is always behind us or else it's guarding the sheep against foxes. I don't understand what they're used for here.'

STOP PRESS!

Gatwick airport closed by snow. Oscar's plane delayed. Tours London. Buys a portable typewriter with earnings from his interview. Sells his own clothes. Poncho now in Bawtry, woven belts in Leeds and London. Oscar wearing British anorak in Peru.

Arctic

Marit Elisabeth Eira

They have amputated me, my land,
our lifegiving rivers
meant to fill the needs
of coming generations
have now to feed robots, the generators!
from a poem by the Sami artist Elle-Hán'sa

To the outsider, the Arctic may seem merely a stretch of wasteland that has no importance for anyone except a few Eskimos and an occasional explorer making his way to the North Pole. But increasingly it is coveted by power groups with different interests.

Russia and North America have many military installations within the Arctic Circle. The shortest route for missiles between Moscow and Washington is across the North Pole. In any future global war the weapons and nuclear submarines concealed there could be decisive.

Oil companies are also moving in to prospect for oil and gas. Some of the world's largest reserves are being found in the Arctic. The resulting wealth will pass mostly to people south of the Arctic.

It is hard to imagine that a single pipeline or military installation could do much harm, but in the Arctic, conditions are precarious. The slightest change can bring great hardship to people who depend on the land and its limited resources for their livelihood. Every square mile counts.

There are many indigenous groups in the Arctic with their own languages and culture. One group is the Sami. Their origins are uncertain but they have lived in the Arctic parts of Sweden, Finland, and Norway for over 2000 years. Known often as Lapps, they prefer the name Sami because 'Lapp' is often used as a term of abuse.

'I live in Masi in the north of Norway. In Sami we spell it Màze,' says Marit Elisabeth Eira. 'I like it best in winter here. There's not so much traffic from tourists. I can ski and sledge and ride the snowscooters. It's a lot of fun.'

The reindeer

The Sami are skilled at using natural resources with care. Many earn their living from fishing or farming, but some herd reindeer.

Marit's parents, grandparents, uncles, aunts and cousins, as well as Marit herself, all own reindeer that are kept together in one herd during the winter. The men work as a team and take it in turns to watch over the animals. They also consult with other groups that share the grazing. Much cooperation is needed.

Marit's family do not own any land, but they have inherited the right to its use from their forefathers. The pattern of herding is well-established. The reindeer are always on the move in search of food. In winter, they dig through the snow for lichen. In summer, they migrate north to the coast for better grazing and to avoid the plagues of mosquitoes on the plateau. En route, they stop in the same place every year for calving. On the way back, there is a special place for breeding.

'There's not so much space nowadays for all the herds,' says Marit's mother. 'It gets taken away bit by bit, and every metre that's lost affects them. Take the main road for instance. It's very good and useful, but it takes land – not just the width of the road, but much more. The reindeer get easily frightened. It's a problem because the breeding grounds are next to the road.'

The family's calving grounds are also under threat from the army who want it as a firing range – the north coast is strategically crucial, for it is the main route of Russian ships and submarines. By law, the state of Norway owns the land. By law, the family have no rights to the land but by tradition and use they do. Though they oppose the takeover, they will probably lose the land.

'I don't like to watch when they kill the reindeer (above) but when Dad wants me to, I have to help. In the autumn, we send some to the slaughterhouse to sell for meat, but we keep what we need for ourselves. We freeze it and dry it and smoke it.'

1. Winter grazing
2. Spring calving
3. Summer grazing
4. Autumn breeding
5. Site of dam
Red lines: Main Roads
Broken line: National Border

'We take as much food (far left) as there's need for when we go to the winter cabin in the mountains. Sometimes my Dad stays for two or three weeks at a time.'

'Sometimes several herds get mixed (left) when they graze too close together and then we have to sort them out in a corral. You can tell from the marks on their ears who owns them. Everyone's marks are written down. I've got my own for my animals. When you're christened, when you get married, you're given reindeer. Then they have calves and you get more reindeer.'

'In the old days, when they were herding, they stayed in the lavvo tent (above). Now it's used for smoking meat. We use parts of the skins to make shoes and clothes, but we sell the big hides to tourists.'

Settling in

'You have to be sixteen before you can drive the snowscooter, but we all have a go. Not so long ago two boys were having a race. One of them crashed and they had to fly him to hospital.'

'We're always playing football. Sometimes it's a bit difficult in the snow. I can ski-jump, and swim, and fish through the ice.'

Officially, there are about 30,000 Sami people in the world who speak the Sami language. Some say there are many more but because of outside pressures they will not admit to being Sami.

Marit has felt such pressure when Norwegians have called her rude names but she likes to call herself a Sami. It helps that she lives in a district where everyone else is Sami and that she does school lessons in Sami. Norwegian is her second language. She can also take time off from school when necessary to work with the Sami reindeer.

At the same time, Marit does not want to be different. Television shows her the latest trends. She no longer wears Sami dress except on special occasions. She prefers the pop group Abba to Sami music. She chews gum by the packet.

The snowscooter has had an even greater impact. Before, the family was

'My mum makes our Sami clothes. Mum and Dad find them easy to wear. When they were young, they wore the costume every day. But we children don't want to put it on too often. It's a lot of work and it's not so comfortable for ordinary wear.'

'This is our house in Masi. We've also got a house on the coast but it burnt down last summer.'

'I wear my costume (bottom) for special occasions like this christening or Sunday church. It's nice.'

nomadic, living in tents while following the reindeer on skis and sledges. Today, the men can reach the most distant herd in a few hours.

'Each working man has to have a snowscooter so he can get about. It's very expensive, like running a car. But it means Dad gets back when he's not working with the reindeer.'

More and more, Masi is becoming a regular base for Marit's family. A tourist centre, an art centre, a new wing of the school and a swimming pool have all been opened recently.

'I wouldn't like to leave Masi. When I'm older I'll work in the shop or with the reindeer,' says Marit. But her mother has a different view. 'The children are living in nice houses now, there's electricity and central heating, they're driving cars, they won't want to work with the reindeer. They're getting urbanised.'

The dam

1968
Plans announced for new dam to make electricity. Valley and Masi threatened with flooding.

1970
Demonstrations in Masi. Banners confront visiting officials — 'We will not move'. 'We came here first'. 'No to flooding the village'. The offers of compensation turned down by families. Memories of evacuation during war when houses burnt down by Nazis.

1973
Parliament declares Masi safe from flooding.

1978
Parliament approves new plans for damming Alta river below Masi. Opposition from groups across the country concerned with nature conservation, Sami rights, and Norway's development options.

1979-1981
Demonstrations against the dam. 'Elva Skal Leve! — The River Shall Live!' Sami go on hunger strike. Hundreds set up camp on site. People chain themselves to bulldozers when construction work begins. 600 police flown in. Arrests. Court cases. The country split in two — should the majority ride roughshod over the few? Should the few prevent improvements for the many? Specialist reports question effectiveness of dam in producing required power. Alternative sources of supply available without the dam.

1982
Norway's Supreme Court gives final ruling in favour of dam. Attempt to blow up bridge on site blows up a Sami man instead. Sympathy for Sami people on decline in Norway. The Sami always seem under pressure.

24

Marit in Britain

DAYS 1 AND 2
Heavy snow in Masi. Sunshine and blossom in UK. 'How can you have such beautiful trees?' Green shrubs on roundabouts. 'We could all climb in and hide there.' No such things in Masi. Groans from Sarah at rush-hour traffic, fascination for Marit. But soon a feeling of claustrophobia, hemmed in by lorries and houses. 'I'd die if I lived in a city.' Notices every horse, on pub signs, in trailers, on TV. 'When am I going to ride?' Beautiful old stone cottages. 'Why do you build in cement?' All wooden in Norway.

DAYS 3 AND 4
Shopping centre. Up and down lifts till police tell her to leave. Apparently a bomb scare. Speedway. At interval in pits to meet Dave Allen and other Superthorne Panthers. Marit over the moon. 'I was nearly sick, my heart was so high. All the boys in Masi are always talking about him.'

DAYS 5 AND 6
Huge picnic at horse trials. Horses, horses, horses. To Leeds for interview, no nerves. Lassoos Sarah first go, pulls her to the floor. Afternoon at riding school. 'The best, best thing of all.' Added excitement with trip to circus, meeting Lawrence the Clown.

DAYS 7 AND 8
Morning in bed exhausted. Meet Travellers and Romany family — Mrs. Herring asks us into her home. Explains had to move from a site two weeks ago, given notice this morning to quit present place, single Council site already overcrowded. Travel by train to London, Marit gazes at passing fields. 'Why can't the Travellers be given just a bit of space? Why are they treated like dogs? We Sami are better off.' Half-hearted sight-seeing. Longing to get home for Easter.

Rivers
Abdul Latif

The clouds array themselves against me,
The lightning paints in golden flashes,
The river speeds along swollen with rain,
In the lightning I see for a moment a golden picture
But never see it again.

boatman's river song, Bangladesh

Rivers make up only a tiny amount of the water in the world – the equivalent of a jugful in a large sized swimming pool. But rivers have always been very important. Many early civilisations grew up around rivers – in Egypt, Mesopotamia, India and China. Many capital cities straddle a major river.

Like the veins in our bodies, rivers are part of human survival, not only as a source of unsalted water for drinking, cooking and washing, but as a source of valuable food such as fish. Land that seems useless can produce a wealth of crops with the help of irrigation or floodwater.

Because river water gives life, it is used in many religions for prayers and blessing. But it can also bring death, for it carries diseases – typhoid, trachoma, bilharzia, river blindness, dysentery, malaria. Millions of children and adults die from these each year; millions more are ill for the rest of their lives.

Rivers have also acted as roadways for traders, explorers, and conquerors. Merchant adventurers from Europe used them to penetrate many countries. Three hundred years ago, they settled along the banks of the Bengal rivers, an area that was rich in produce. The British in particular shipped out goods by the ton and brought in soldiers and rulers.

Ruled by the British until 1947, East Bengal then became part of Pakistan. In 1971 it fought for independence as Bangladesh. A land of rivers, it has 8,000 kilometres of waterways and the largest river delta in the world. One major river is the Meghna, with thousands of villages along its banks – including Barudi where Abdul Latif lives. The river gives Latif the means to earn a living.

A day's work

Latif has handled a river boat since he was eight. Today he is about fourteen, and his elderly parents rely on him for the money he can earn from the boat.

Each morning at six o'clock, Latif and his brother Jalil set off from the village in their boat. They keep close to the bank where there is less current, calmer water, and more wind. If the wind is behind them, they sail downstream; if not, they have to row or pole for about an hour and a half until they come to Baidya Bazar.

Here they tie up their boat and wait for passengers. Other boats alongside are also for hire, so they must compete for business. In the rainy season, there is lots of work. The paths and fields are flooded so people have to hire boats in order to reach their villages. At harvest time, too,

there are crops to carry. For about three months, Latif can earn up to one hundred taka a day (about £2.50). From September onwards, the demand for boats goes down as the river subsides.

'If people can walk, why would they pay a boatman?' says Latif. 'For two months, in February and March, it is really bad when the river is very lean. At this time of year people have very little money and find it difficult to get employment, so they can't afford to take boats. We just stay at home then. There's no cash to earn. We spend what we've saved, or else we borrow money.'

After a day's work, Latif gives all his earnings to his father. He keeps only a little himself for pocket expenses, like sweets and snacks for lunch.

'What I like most is to hold the rudder and sail along. The boat goes more urgently. We are always passing other boats. In calm weather we can take as many as twenty people and they pay three taka each. In rough weather we take less and charge more. If they won't pay we don't take them. We always want to take as many passengers as possible.'

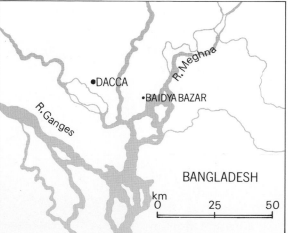

'There are so many rivers in Bangladesh, but it's not possible to get lost. We always know the way. I went with my brother Rustam fifty miles upstream to fetch a load of yarn. Once I rowed twenty miles to a town the other side of the river. It took half a day.'

'There's a meal at home in the evening. One of the women does the cooking and my mother does the serving. We always have curry and there's usually fresh fish from the river.'

'I usually sleep on the boat perhaps twenty nights out of thirty. Somebody has to guard the boat, and I usually stay alone. Sometimes I ask my friend Ibu to come to the boat and then he will come that night after he's been to school.'

Meghna, the River of Cloud

From the high Himalayas to the Bay of Bengal a network of rivers pours down, bringing life to the people of Bangladesh. As the snows melt, so the waters move, bringing mud and soil and goodness; as the monsoon starts, the rains swell the rivers further.

'They say you can roam all of Bangladesh on the Meghna. You can even go abroad down this river. But is it possible to go so far on my small boat into such an enormous ocean?' asks Latif.

The meaning of *megh* is cloud, and the Meghna river depends for its water on rainclouds and the distant cloudland of mountains and melting snows. In June and July, the river begins to rise, spreading water across the land beyond the banks of the river.

'We don't have such huge floods in our region. When the water floods, it doesn't harm people. In fact, it is very good for our people. Without the water coming in over the land, the padi can't grow in our village, the jute can't grow. Without water, there are many problems'.

Yet there are problems in times of flooding. A lot of work has to be done in the fields, and food is sometimes scarce since the crops have still to be harvested. As a result, poorer people become tired and ill. Also precious farm land is washed away as the river changes its course – the owners lose their means of growing food. A few years ago, the police station at Baidya Bazar fell into the water when the river bank collapsed beneath it.

In the monsoon, the landscape changes to look like a lake. Roads, bridges, fields and football pitches disappear under water. But the fishing is good, the crops can grow, and business for boatmen booms.

'There's no better river than the Meghna,' says Latif. Better or worse, he has little choice where he can earn his living – he will probably depend for the rest of his life on the Meghna.

'We grow padi (below) once a year when the new water floods in from the river. We harvest enough to eat for four months and then we must buy from the market. Not everyone has land, especially the poorest families. My father used to be like that until he was given some land by some people who left to go to India.'

'The water hyacinths may look nice, but they trap a lot of boats and damage the crops when the fields flood.'

River boats

To the visitor, the boats of Bangladesh are an impressive sight as they silently sweep along the river. They number about 250,000, from the smallest dinghy to huge ketches that sail out to sea. Each is hand-made from wood by craftsmen with years of experience. They are known as 'country' boats and are driven by wind and human muscle. About 2,500 steamers and launches also run on the larger rivers.

Many of the boats carry passengers but they also carry cargo, especially during the harvest when crops are cut. Jute, rice, sugar-cane, vegetables and tobacco are carried in millions of tons from farm to village, from village to town, from market-place to market-place for trading. Some crops, such as tea and jute, are produced with cheap labour and shipped out of the country by foreign companies to sell for more money elsewhere.

Latif would like to do some trading, just as his brothers do. They carry cargoes for other people but they also buy and sell cloth and yarn for themselves at a small profit. All the brothers, including Latif, are busy on market days. Latif's boat can carry a ton at a time. He takes sacks of rice, bundles of cloth, baskets of dried fish, even some goats and a cow. The market seems very crowded after the space of the river.

Latif has never been to school, apart from a day when he ran away. He cannot see the point. He remembers all the things he needs to know without having to write them down, and at school he wouldn't earn money to support his parents. It's not as though he were ignorant.

'If you asked me a thousand questions, I could still tell you things that you wouldn't dream of asking. I know all this because I've been on the river since I fell out of my mother's womb.'

(Above) 'This convoy is bringing padi from Sylhet. If they travel together, it's safer so that a bunch of bandits can't attack them. The bandits beat up the boatmen, rob them of their goods, burn their boats, they do all kinds of damage. Our boat has never been robbed but a neighbour's boat was robbed.'

(Above right) 'In the rainy season, boats can go right up to the weekly market along some small canals, but you have to work very hard to get there. They come from far away places – they bring molasses from Savar, padi from Sylhet. Other people bring cloth, fish, a whole variety of things. Aluminium crockery, fruit, many brands of cigarettes, spices for the curry.'

The Kiwi (left) was built in Dumbarton, Scotland, and shipped out in parts to Calcutta at the time of the British Raj. There she was reassembled in 1930. 'I love looking at the different boats, but I wouldn't want to work on a steamer. I'd rather be my own boss with my own boat. Engines and petrol are too expensive.'

'We always buy chillies from the same man. For five or six years, he's been trading in chillies. With my own boat, I could travel quite far to trade.'

Latif in Britain

Latif arrives London Airport, accompanied by Shireen the interpreter. Drive home. Latif stares out of car window at first views of London. Big Ben and River Thames. 'Don't you have any rivers?' Women in high heels. 'It's weird. Why do they walk on spikes?' Shock at the price of shoes — two weeks earnings for him.

DAY 2
Mild weather but icy for Latif — wrapped in layers of clothes. Drive along empty country lane. 'The king of this country must be very rich if he can afford to build expensive roads through nowhere.' In Bangladesh, tarmac roads a luxury that get washed away by floods every year. A hundred questions about land 'We can get three crops a year from the same piece of land. We have rivers and plenty of help. You have tractors and rain.'

DAY 3
Football. Friends assume they'll have to show Latif how to play. He shows them instead. Scores several times. Speed king and twice as fit as anybody else. Other visitors think of him as poor and therefore a bit slow, but he's learned to drive in a day and buzzes across the field in our car at every possible moment.

DAY 4
Latif thinks TV boring and food strange and tasteless. He finds a rusty nail. 'This is the only thing that's the same between your house and my house, perhaps between all of Britain and Bangladesh.' Shopping for presents to take home. In toy department, nothing appeals except a football. In hardware, goes for torches, a mirror for his mother, some cooking ladles — useful things. Stares at a bike — same price as his boat, about £100.

DAY 5

Fishing on the River Nene with David. Just the two, no one to translate. Caught a huge pike — at least Latif did on David's rod. Jumped around in excitement. David thought Latif was trying to say that in his religion or something they didn't kill things. So David threw the fish back. Latif didn't stop him because he thought that maybe in Britain people didn't eat fish. Both miserable when found each wanted to keep it.

DAY 6

Sports centre. Latif swims like a fish. Totally at home in water. Is amazed by the girls showing so much flesh. 'At home, the girls don't swim any more after they're ten or eleven. Even the boys don't fool around once they're working men.'

DAY 7

TV interview, Leeds. Very expressive, but says his mind keeps blanking out — all that equipment! 'This television company is even richer than the king of this country.' His English now includes the word 'studio'. Also dog, duck, horse, thank you, loose, cold, chocolate, thank God, football, no.

DAY 8

Bus tour of London — all the city sights. Then to East End. To Latif, no difference from posh West End, all houses and traffic. But a chance to meet others from Bangladesh. Very at home — real food and real language at last. Hears about problems — poor housing, fewer jobs, attacks by white people. Visits karate class. 'They have to learn karate to protect themselves.'

DAY 9

Last day — at school! Questions. Questions. Questions. Lunch. Football. Fishing stories. Building a model river boat. Two girls dress themselves in saris. Laughter. 'I'm very happy here. But then I stop and think — why am I laughing? It'll all be over soon.'

Rain Forest

Pauline Bala

*After she has walked for one month, she suddenly
    comes to the burnt forest edge of a padi field.
She stands on the flat log placed there, a log
    carved with triangles marking the number of
    heads taken.
She looks out across in all directions…*

from a traditional Kelabit song

By the time you read this page, an area of tropical
rain forest the size of one hundred football pitches
will have been cut down across the world. When
the rain forest vanishes, so do hundreds of types of
insects, plants, and animals. It is the richest
environment in the world and is vital both to
wildlife and human beings.

Each year, thousands of rain forest plants are
tested for medical research – they can help cure
diseases such as leukaemia and other types of
cancer. They can also provide new varieties of
food when crops elsewhere are ruined by disease.

The tropical rain forest in Borneo is fast
disappearing. Families need firewood for cooking
and warmth; poor people clear patch after patch to
grow food; companies demand land for rubber and
pepper plantations, and foreign countries cry out
for timber to make pulp for paper.

Many different groups live in the rain forest of
Sarawak on the Malaysian side of Borneo. The
most remote group is perhaps the Kelabit, who
number about 3,000. No one is sure of their origin,
though their megalithic stones go back hundreds
and hundreds of years.

'My father found one when he was clearing the
jungle,' says Pauline Bala. 'It's my favourite place
for playing. There's a design on the rock of a man
slaying an enemy. A renowned headhunter. My
grandfather was also a famous headhunter.'

For Pauline, the Kelabit Highlands are home.
For the outsider, they are hard to reach – a three
week walk through dense jungle or a flight that is
frequently cancelled because of rain. Aeroplanes
can land on the grass airstrip only when it is dry.

The longhouse

In 1963, war broke out along the border between Malaysia and Indonesia just a few miles from Pauline's longhouse. Her father was mobilised by British troops to fight for three years. At one time bullets strafed the longhouse. Kelabit elders recommended evacuation, but the families refused to move.

Nine families live now at Pa'umor, a village settlement that stands on its own in the rain forest. There is only one building, the longhouse, which is more than seventy metres long and thirty metres wide. Each family has its own section with areas for cooking, washing, eating and sleeping. There are no walls between each family's 'house' – it is all open plan. At the front, a long, covered verandah gives space for games, gatherings and daily church services.

The families in the longhouse sometimes join up to help each other with hunting, farming, or building. An elected headman supervises the arrangements and sorts out disputes.

It took Pauline's family four months to build their part of the house. Her father cut down the trees for planks. 'The whole structure is wooden except for the zinc roof,' says Pauline. 'The house is built on stilts to avoid the wet ground.' Pigs, chickens, and hunting dogs live in a yard at the back.

Often, a whole longhouse shifts its site when the surrounding land is no longer good for farming. Pa'umor moved to its present position in 1956. 'Our house will stand for 35 years,' predicts Pauline. But already there is talk of moving closer to Bario, the main Kelabit centre on the other side of the river.

On weekdays, the longhouse is often empty. The parents are out in the fields, the children away at school. But at weekends the longhouse hums with activity. 'When we're home, we love to sing and we use guitars. We chit-chat, make cakes, play games. But there aren't many girls my age at Pa'umor.'

'We make balloons out of our sarongs and float downstream like ducks. The word for river is "Pa". Our longhouse is next to the river, so it's called Pa'umor.'

'My granny lives with us. She still has her tattoos. In the old days, if a woman didn't have any tattoos, she wouldn't be considered noble or brave, and she wouldn't have any suitors for marriage. I wouldn't like to have tattoos, but I like long earlobes.'

(Right) 'Our house is No. 6. We're the largest family. You can tell each person's house by the square wooden fireplace where we do the cooking. When there are guests in the longhouse, each family prepares a dish. My father often cooks it. It's good living in a longhouse. It means we all share. But sometimes I wish we had walls between each house. It can be embarrassing when everyone is watching.'

Fruits of the forest

'There's nowhere we can buy meat, so we have to find our own in the jungle. Wild boar, deer, monkey. Usually only the men go hunting. This time, two deer were heading towards us but my uncle missed and shot a tree-trunk instead.'

'We're helping my mother plant maize and groundnuts on the farm. She and my father do most of the work. We grow rice, sweet potatoes, tapioca, and lots of fruit.'

'My mother and my grandmother know a lot about the jungle – where to pick things, how to make things.' Pauline's knowledge is more to do with school subjects, like Malaysian history and languages. Her knowledge of the rain forest is limited.

'I'm frightened when I'm in the jungle alone. But I know how to search for food, like fruits, all kinds of shoots, and mushrooms.'

The rain forest gives the family an abundance of food. Game from hunting, fish from the rivers, a range of fruit and vegetables. There is wild honey and salt springs to make into salt. Even firelighters are provided by the resin from certain trees and there is plenty of wood for the stove.

A few years ago, the rivers dried up from lack of rain. Pauline's father was hunting deep in the forest one day when

he found a small stream. All through the summer, he went back to check it, but the stream kept flowing. He checked it the following year. The stream was still flowing. So he staked out a small valley as his farm, then cut down the trees and burnt them. He diverted the stream to his new plot and planted padi. With irrigation, he had a bumper harvest. The farm now produces maize, groundnuts, tapioca, fruit and sweet potatoes.

Of all the things in the tropical rain forest, Pauline loves the pink orchid most. She does not like snakes, but they do little damage to humans compared with insects that carry disease – the mosquito, the cockroach, the fly. 'There are lots of insects in the jungle. In the evening, when the cicada starts singing, we know it's time to go home. Sometimes the noise is so loud, it's troublesome. It stops me from going to sleep.'

'My father is throwing the fishing net. We are groping for fish. We dig our hands into the mud and feel around. The fish live in holes in the mud. They're grass carp. Sometimes we fry them, we make fish soup, and we roast them in bamboo. We smoke fish, too, if we catch a great deal.'

(Left) 'These are sticks of salt wrapped in jungle leaves and tied with rottan. Bamboo – behind me – is used for all sorts of things. For roofing, for building fences and bridges, for making fire tongs, fish traps and mugs. We also eat the young shoots as a vegetable.'

41

Leaving home

In term-time on Sunday afternoons, Pauline, her three younger sisters, and several other children leave Pa'umor longhouse to walk back to school in Bario. It takes two hours to walk through the rain forest but the path is wide and well-worn. A bridge across the river is made from oil drums left by British troops.

Bario is the hub of life, with a shop, a health centre, the airstrip and two schools. Before 1946, there was no school in the Kelabit Highlands and not one Kelabit was literate. Then a primary school started. A secondary school opened in 1967. By 1980, some forty students had passed into university.

'My grandparents can't read or write,' says Pauline. 'My father can. He had to walk for weeks to get to school. There were no planes in those days. Now two of my sisters are at university in Kuala Lumpur, and my only brother is in college. They take the plane to get there. It's expensive, so they don't come home very often, but the government does help with the costs.'

In the last thirty years, the changes have been dramatic for the Kelabit community. Most important of all has been conversion to Christianity. In 1973, a powerful religious revival swept the Bario school. Schoolchildren persuaded parents and teachers to turn fully to God, leaving old beliefs behind.

Having lived for centuries in the security and isolation of their rain forest, the Kelabit people are now moving out to face the world. Their success and adaptability are not without pain. Those that leave for higher education sometimes never return, except for the occasional visit. They grow used to city life and the comfort of earning wages.

Those that are left behind continue to farm, for there is no alternative work in the highlands. As the young leave, so the old lose the chance of help. It is a small and isolated community that in the past has depended on its own resources.

(Far left) 'There are sixteen boys and twenty girls in my class. The red band shows I'm a prefect. I'm twelve. Next year I start secondary school. I want to be a teacher so I can stay here and teach. But I'll have to leave to be trained.'

'All the girls from Pa'umor sleep at one end of the dormitory. I always put my sisters to bed. Sometimes I want to go out to play, but I have to stay and look after them.'

The road to Bario from Pa'umor. In the last twenty years, Bario has become the main Kelabit centre with its airstrip, schools and permanent padi fields.

'It's not possible to get lost. We've known this path all our lives. Along the way, we eat berries and hide in the bushes. Half-way, there's a resting place called "the bus-stop". We often stop there to play. We climb trees like monkeys, we chase each other, we play all sorts of games. And if we're thirsty, that's where we drink some water.'

Pauline in Britain

DAY 1
Arrives London Airport with interpreter/cousins Lucy and David. Tours London in pouring rain and gloom. 'So many lights, so bright.'

DAY 2
Countryside. Shocked at leafless trees. 'Poor trees, are they *all* dead? At home, all our trees are green all the time.' Running along the beach on the Suffolk coast. 'The waves are so big. Where does all the water come from?'

DAY 3
'Your trains are longer than our longhouses. Your houses are not on stilts. Why not? They're strange — all brick and concrete.'

DAY 4
York Cathedral. 'Is the king of this country Christian? Oh praise the Lord!' Flying Tortoise Children's Theatre perform *Freddie Superflea*. Pauline joins in. 'At home, we do a long dance. It has many beautiful movements. In the old days, the women danced out of the longhouse in a line to welcome home their husbands. They rejoiced to see them alive after a head-hunting trip.'

DAY 5
Loves the BP petrol signs — her father's initials, Bala Palaba. Names very important. His means 'Frequent News'. As young man, always hitting community headlines. Grandmother's name, 'Sea of Life'. Pauline to take new name when has first child and when becomes a grandmother. At each stage, must reflect her character. 'Quiet Brightness' seems right for now.

DAY 6
Visit to school. Art class. Liked the weaving. Very easy. Weaves mats at home from forest leaves. Quickly accepted by classmates. Quietly shared their work. Fascinated by informal methods of teaching.

44

DAY 7

National Railway Museum, York, with John Gerard. Special visit allowed into royal carriages. HM King Edward VII's saloon, 1903. Discreetly lavish. Sits down at King's dressing table. 'I am the king. No, not the queen. I don't want to be a woman. I wish I'd been born a boy.'

DAY 8

TV interview. Pauline does hornbill dance, all feathers. Boxes of Borneo insects. Loud jungle noise. Toad and cicada jump round set, scaring Pauline and Sarah. Boxes of Borneo produce — the chew in chewing gum, pepper, and wood for furniture. Also Malaysian rubber — elastic bands, rubber gloves, swimming caps, windscreen wipers. To grow such rubber on plantations, tropical rain forest being cut down. Amazing environment gone forever all for a rubber band.

DAY 9

No wish to stay in the urban jungle. 'There are so many people here! Wherever one goes, it's so crowded.'

Browsing through Borneo book, found instructions from Sarawak elder in Pauline's region:

"Should you leave home
And go down river for foreign
    places,
Please do not stay put,
But come back to your people,
Like a tame hornbill returning
    to its owner.
Return to the village where
    you belong
To rejoin your father and
the whole lot of his people
Of the longhouse."

Islands
Iagan MacInnes

Eriskay... of the speckled knolls and the bright white strands; 'tis there one finds strong men who are not afraid when the sea rises, and kindly, tuneful, diligent women who sing more sweetly than the birds on the trees.

Fr. Allan McDonald, priest to Eriskay 1893–1905

To the romantic person, an island is a place that is always unspoilt by modern life or the presence of other people. Dreams are conjured up of empty white beaches, blue lagoons, maybe some pirate treasure. Each year, thousands of people pursue such dreams by taking an island holiday. There are tens of thousands of islands to choose from.

Nobody knows exactly how many islands there are in the world. In the British Isles, the figures vary from 1,100 to 2,000. The largest group is the Hebrides with about 500, but less than 100 have people living on them.

Although parts of the Hebrides are made from the oldest rock in the world, they were first inhabited only 9,000 years ago, when the climate changed from extreme cold to warm, allowing people to settle. Others followed – the Picts, the Scots, the Celts, the Vikings, and Scottish chiefs from the mainland known as the Lords of the Isles.

Unlike dreams, life on an island can be harsh. In the nineteenth century, small-scale farmers were evicted by landlords to make way for more profitable sheepfarming. Many died from famine; others were forced to sail to Australia and North America. Today, the islands are disturbed by the presence of NATO armed forces and a missile base.

Iagan MacInnes lives on the island of Eriskay in the Outer Hebrides. He speaks Gaelic, the language of the islands that has stayed alive while English has spread on the mainland. His schoolfriends call him John Gerard, but his family uses the Gaelic Iagan. He can trace his ancestors back for generations, always as island inhabitants.

At the age of eleven, John Gerard has been to the mainland only twice.

Born on an island

In 1841, only eighty people lived on the tiny island of Eriskay. There was little to attract the newcomer, with its rocky earth and gale-swept banks so that hardly a tree could survive. Yet by 1851, the population had swollen to over 400 people. They had fled from neighbouring islands, cleared off their land by greedy landlords who wanted more space for sheep.

Eriskay gave them refuge, though life was very hard. With the help of children and grandchildren, as well as each other, the families of Eriskay survived, including the MacInnes family.

Today, 226 people live on Eriskay, but their chances of work are limited, despite a tradition of fishing. 'If I stayed on the island,' says John Gerard, 'I could be a fisherman, a builder, a ferryman, even the priest or teacher. But I want to fly an aeroplane. For that, I'll have to leave the island.' Already, 247 people who were born on Eriskay live elsewhere.

John Gerard's father joined the merchant navy at sixteen. 'Sometimes, there's a place on television like India or Africa, and my Dad says he was there. I feel very proud.' But after some years, he came back to settle on Eriskay.

Others come back to be buried, for they cannot forget their island, however far they have gone. The cemetery stands on the edge of the island overlooking the sea that claims its share of lives. In World War II, three bodies were washed ashore from a torpedoed ship. Two years ago, an Eriskay man was washed off his boat and drowned. John Gerard's uncle – John – was killed at sea.

Those that remain on the island attend a ceremony every year to bless the fishing boats and pray for safety. With government limits and smaller catches, the fishing gets harder and harder.

'I know all the people on the island. Lots of them are cousins. Only four people don't have any relatives at all. The big group on the left all belong to the MacKinnons. They're the family that own six fishing boats. There aren't many men in the picture because they're away fishing. The older boys are away too, at school on another island.'

48

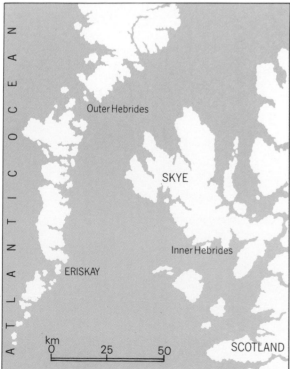

'Lots of people from the island are buried here, including my granny and grandfather, and some of my uncles and aunts. I visit them every Sunday. It was my great-great grandfather who came to the island first.'

(Left) 'The fishing boats are out all week. They have to get lots of fish. When there are gales, we feel scared, especially my mum. Often we go down to meet the boats when they come in on Fridays. My dad used to fish but he got ill and had to stop.'

Bound by the sea

On Eriskay, the longest car ride takes only ten minutes, but it costs four pounds fifty to take the car by ferry to the neighbouring island to fill up with petrol. There are few places to cycle, one football pitch, and only the cold sea for swimming. Gales can blow for days.

John Gerard lives in a council house and goes to the local school. At fourteen he will have to leave Eriskay to go to a senior school on another island.

'I wish there were more people on this island to work with and play with,' he laments. But he still finds plenty to do. There is the long silver beach where Bonnie Prince Charlie landed, with its caves and rocks to explore. There are whelks to collect on the seashore, with a sackful selling for ten pounds in summer and twenty three pounds in winter. A youth club and disco meant entertainment until the hall caved in. The islanders must raise £17,000 themselves to qualify for a grant to build a community centre.

Until three years ago, John Gerard's family had to hire both a boat and a taxi to shop on another island. Now a cooperative shop has been organised and financed by the islanders with local government help. Everything has to be shipped from the mainland. Food costing £1 in England costs £1.20 on Eriskay.

For those with dreams and plenty of money, the island of Eriskay was for sale recently at a price of £200,000. Those living on Eriskay felt the island had little economic value and put in a bid of £5,000. This was turned down by the owners, an estate syndicate. No one else has bought it – dreams can be too expensive.

'I like chips and steaks the best. But we're always having fried fish that my dad gets fresh off the boats. I wish we could have fish fingers but they're too expensive.'

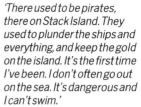

'There used to be pirates, there on Stack Island. They used to plunder the ships and everything, and keep the gold on the island. It's the first time I've been. I don't often go out on the sea. It's dangerous and I can't swim.'

'We dig a trench and turn the soil onto a line of seaweed (left). Then my mother puts in the potatoes. The seaweed helps them grow. It's a good fertiliser. We fetch it from the beach in baskets on the Eriskay ponies. And then you just put a fence round it all. It's called a lazy bed. That's about all we can grow. Sometimes some swede, maybe a cabbage patch, or carrots.'

'We've made a model of the Britannia—that's one of the Eriskay fishing boats. We did it in school as part of a fishing project. Our teacher comes from Eriskay. There are six of us in our class.'

Changing Ways

IN THE PAST

'If I got washed up on the island like my great-great-grandfather did, first of all I'd build a shelter with local stones. I'd get driftwood on the shore for the rafters and then I'd dig up some turf to cover the roof. Then I'd get something to eat. I'd go down to the seashore and get all the winkles and that. I'd cut peat and burn it for warmth. And then I'd plant some potatoes — provided I'd brought some with me.'

IN THE PRESENT

'There's virtually no peat left today so coal comes once a year by boat for everyone on Eriskay. We keep ours in a bunker at the back of the house. We've also got electric fires and heaters. There are a few crofts on the island, but nobody lives in them anymore. They're too cold and leaky. For our house, the bricks were brought in from the mainland, and all the tiles and timber. We get our clothes and records and games — even some of our furniture - through mail order catalogues. I wish I could have a bicycle.'

IN THE FUTURE

'There's mass everyday in the church, but I go just on Sundays. Everyone on Eriskay helped to build it in 1903. The fishermen said that the money they got from a day's fishing would go towards funds for the church. They said their prayers and went out in the fishing boats. That day, they caught the best catch they ever had.' Though help may come from God and nowadays from government subsidy, the islanders of Eriskay face a difficult future. As fishing declines, many must find other ways of making money. The possibilities on the island are few, so many more may have to leave to find work elsewhere.

New Sights

OCTOBER — DECEMBER
Strike on at Yorkshire TV. John Gerard and full supporting family's visit cancelled. Agony waiting till new date set. 'Will it ever happen?' This time just John Gerard, sister and parents. Two days travel to Leeds.

DAY 1
No traffic islands on Eriskay. Nor any flats or office blocks. Visit to York railway museum. 'I'm not very interested in trains. I don't get much chance to see them. I like the *Mallard* best — it's the fastest steam train in the world.' Restaurant meal at night. Delicious Italian dishes. Takes four menus back as souvenirs for brothers and sisters left behind on Eriskay — no restaurant there.

DAY 2
TV interview. 'There was a girl from Borneo at the studios called Pauline. She was also doing an interview. Hers came first and then I had mine.' Everyone thought he was great. Even John Gerard surprised how much Hebridean seaweed part of our daily

lives — as alginate. Glaze on liquorice, stops sediment forming in squash, keeps oil in ice cream mixed with milk, provides gel in tins of pet food.

DAY 3
Leeds United. 'I got quite a lot of autographs and I even trained with some of United's players.' Proved himself at heading. On to Rowntrees factory. 'All that smell of chocolate.' A million Kit-Kat bars pounding out a week, day and night. 'Don't you ever go to bed? How do you keep awake? We don't have shift work where I live.'

Desert

Fatimettou mint Deye

*Familiar landmarks appear to you shining in a
   blaze.
Their beauty delights the eyes of those who see
   them, if the hand of rain adorns them with
   tender herbs which blend the beauty of their
   whiteness with verdure.
That is my land, which I love and long for.*
poem of Mauritania

When asked to name a desert, most people say the
Sahara. As the largest desert in the world, it has
attracted adventurers and travellers for centuries.
Their journeys grow more and more strange – a
vicar pushing a wheelbarrow, actors giving shows,
a prime minister's son losing his way in a car rally.

In the past, it also attracted the French, who
conquered and colonised vast areas. As they
handed back countries, they left behind systems of
trade, frontiers and governments that often had
little to do with the wishes or needs of the people
who lived there. Mauritania achieved independence from France in 1960. Its frontiers run south to
the fertile banks of the Senegal river and north to
the desert wastelands. As a result, the population
is half 'black African' and half 'white Moor'. They
have limited contact.

Traditionally, the Moors have lived in the
north, at the western end of the Sahara desert.
Traders, camel breeders, and tribal nomads, they
also own palm-groves. The Adrar region, where
Fatimettou lives, is famous for its dates.

'My grandmother harvests the dates every
August,' says Fatimettou. 'That's the best time,
when the palm-groves are very green, and
thousands of people come from all over the
region.' As members of the same tribe, they have
tribal rights to the dates, which are rich in sugar,
protein, fat, and minerals. 'They stay for a month
or two, and then they leave, and we're by
ourselves again. I don't often visit this palm grove,
even with a friend. I'm not allowed into the dunes.
There's always the danger of strangers passing by.'

The Sheikh

'Hard work, honesty, courtesy, belief in God – these are the important qualities of people, not wealth, or tribe, or skin colour,' explains the Sheikh. 'There is a religious saying that all people are equal. I believe it. In colonial times, I bought slaves simply to set them free. I gave my daughter of noble birth in marriage to a former slave.'

(Far left) 'My uncle gives all the directions. Here, the brothers are digging a well in the village. In this summer heat, we need a lot of water to drink.'

The village where Fatimettou lives is called El Maden. It was started fifteen years ago by her great-uncle, the Sheikh, a Muslim religious leader of great learning. He had stone houses built for his family and followers, who are known as 'the brothers'. During the day they work in the fields; at night they pray. They chant the name of God for many hours. 'I like chanting the name of God,' says Fatimettou. 'Those who know the Qur'an – the Holy Book of Islam – and those who live correctly will go to heaven.'

The Sheikh comes from a wealthy and noble family. As a 'saint', he also receives from his followers money and many gifts – once he was given two Landrovers. Yet he spends as much as he receives on helping others, giving hospitality, and developing the land around El Maden for the community's benefit.

'People who live in the desert must help each other. No man may refuse another help,' says the Sheikh. 'A rich man particularly has many obligations to look after others. If he does, he can achieve many important things.'

He has purchased palm-groves and large areas of desert. With his disciples as the workforce, he has dug wells, installed pumps, built dams, and rapidly increased the productivity of the land. He has also given away some forty plots of land to people in the community to farm themselves. A school and small shop were recently opened.

'The Sheikh takes care of everything,' says Fatimettou's grandmother. 'He has given us life. We give him great respect.'

'I love the gardens of the Sheikh,' says Fatimettou. 'He has made the desert green. We grow beans, groundnuts, tomatoes, carrots as well as fruit and grain. I know every parcel of land, who it belongs to, what everyone is doing. The Sheikh gave my grandmother her own plot.'

(Above left) 'I started Qur'an classes when I was three or four. I go every morning before school, and in the evening. We learn verses from the Qur'an, writing and reciting. Our teacher is very good. He also acts as a blacksmith and helps my uncle with the work.'

A woman's way

The family of Fatimettou consider themselves one of the most noble in the region, at least in name if not in wealth. The behaviour of their children is therefore very important – no shame should come on the family from improper behaviour, especially from a girl.

Fatimettou lives with her grandmother in El Maden and not with her mother in the capital city three hundred miles away. Her grandmother does not consider the city a suitable place for young girls. She also has more experience of life and her opinion counts.

Fatimettou is not expected to work, for there are others in the community to fetch water, prepare the meals, work the land. 'There's not a lot to do here. I walk with my friends in the palm-groves and do things around the house, like making tea or pouring water.' Whenever she can, she willingly helps her grandmother.

Not long ago, girls were married at puberty in order to protect the family's honour. If a girl got pregnant without being married, she would probably be killed. Before marriage, the girls were forcibly fed with milk to make them fat and attractive. In the desert, where life is hard and food limited, a fat woman was the sign of a prosperous family.

Today, much is changing. Many people are moving to towns, and girls have the chance of going to school. 'I want to study right up to senior level,' says Fatimettou. 'I want to be a doctor, to help cure the sick. But I'd have to go to Atar, the capital of the region. I couldn't go alone and my grandmother might not be willing to move with me.'

Although many decisions are made by Fatimettou's elders, the restrictions will begin to fade as she herself grows older. She will probably marry two or three times, for many people divorce and remarry in Mauritania. Not that she feels restricted now, for she already has the freedom to go to school, and to visit her mother in the capital city once a year.

'This is my aunt and her baby who nearly died. She's lost one child already. If a baby dies it's the will of God.' The baby had acute diarrhoea – a major killer of children in the world. A steady diet of clean water and glucose helped to cure the baby.

'Every day, the women make couscous. They are all wives of my uncle, but it's rare in Mauritania for a Moor to have more than one wife at a time. Their children are all my friends. The one in red was magically cured by my uncle from very bad pains in the head. The one facing me was a slave once. The two others are Moors.'

'The best time of day is the early morning when the sun's hardly risen. The hot sun gets on my nerves. At dawn, I sometimes climb up the rocks and look down on the village. Our house is the oblong one, with our storehouse to the right.'

'I love my grandmother very much. She's always taken care of me. I love my mother too. We often hug each other.'

Drawn to the city

Once a year, Fatimettou makes the long journey to Nouakchott, the capital that has become a magnet to Mauritanians. In fifteen years, its population has swollen from 5000 to 250,000. In the early 1970's, nomads came to settle when years of drought had destroyed their herds and flocks. More and more followed. Many became dependent on free milk and food from international charities. Many others stayed for the schools, the shops, and a chance of finding work.

Facilities such as water, houses, and health clinics are limited. Because of a war in the Western Sahara, the government has little money to spend on helping the poor. But people keep on arriving. By 1995, perhaps three-quarters of Mauritania's population will be living in Nouakchott. The movement of people could slow down only if the countryside and small towns are developed – as the Sheikh is doing – so that people can prosper.

Fatimettou stays with her mother in the city. They frequently visit relatives, for family bonds are strong. Her mother is twenty six and works in a bank. Not unusually for the city, she has married four times. Her first husband – Fatimettou's father – left her when she was seventeen.

Some women try to make a living in the city by selling vegetables or cloth or trinkets. The tent acts as a shop. Twenty years ago most Mauritanians were nomadic. Now most of them have settled.

ORGANISATIONS TO CONTACT

Centre for World Development Education (CWDE), 128 Buckingham Palace Road, London SW1W 9SH, tel. 01-730 8332/3 (comprehensive catalogue and stock of publications for all ages).

Local Development Education Centres, for addresses – contact National Association of Development Education Centres, c/o CWDE, tel. 01-730 0972.

Commonwealth Institute, Kensington High Street, London W8 6NQ, tel. 01-602 3052 (library, exhibitions and publications).

FURTHER READING

An asterisk (*) denotes books for older readers and adults.

Mountains
Broad and Alien is the World, Ciro Alegria, Merlin Press, London 1973
Land and Power in South America, Sven Lindquist, Penguin Books, London 1979
New Reference Library: Mountains, Macdonald Educational, London 1980
A new home for Juanita, Michael Pollard, Oxfam
Peru: The Quechua, Michael Sallnow, Basil Blackwell/ILEA, Oxford 1978
Nature's Landscapes: Mountains and People, Iain Bain and Albert McDonald, Wayland, Hove, 1982
Bolivia: Moving to the Future, Oxfam, 1978

Arctic
The Hot Arctic, John Dyson, Heinemann, London 1979
The Lapps, Arthur Spencer, David & Charles, Newton Abbott 1978
Surviving Peoples: Eskimos, Macdonald Educational, London 1979
A Closer Look at Arctic Lands, J. L. Hicks, Hamish Hamilton, London 1976
Eskimo Boy, Bryan and Cherry Alexander, A & C Black, London 1979

Rivers
Water, Sanitation, Health – for all? Anil Agarwal, et al. Earthscan/IIED, London 1981
Bangladesh, B.L.C. Johnson, Heinemann Educ. Books, London 1975
The River Boats of Bangladesh, Oxfam 1977
Folk Tales of Bangladesh, P.C. Roy Chaudhury, Sterling/Independent Publishing Company 1982, Soma Books, 38 Kennington Lane, London SE11 4LF
Nature's Landscapes: Rivers and People, Tom Browne, Wayland, Hove 1982
Photographs from Bangladesh, (with teacher's notes) ILEA London 1981, ILEA Learning Materials Service

Rain Forest
Mulu, Robin Hanbury-Tenison, Weidenfeld & Nicolson, London 1980
World Within, Tom Harrisson, Cresset Press, London 1959
Surviving Peoples: Amazon Indians, Macdonald Educational, London 1980
Folk Tales of Malaysia, Zakaria bin Hitam, Sterling Independent Publishing Company, 1979, Soma Books (address as before)
A Closer Look at Jungles, Joyce Pope, Hamish Hamilton, London 1978

Islands
The Making of the Crofting Community, James Hunter, John Donald, Edinburgh 1976
The Hebrides, W.H. Murray, Heinemann, London 1966
The Shell Book of the Islands of Britain, D. Booth & D. Perrott, Guideway/Windward, London 1981
The World of an Island, P. Coxon, Faber & Faber, London 1977
Islanders, Chick Chalmers, A & C Black, London 1979

Desert
A Study of Female Life in Mauritania, Barbara Abeille, 1979, available from Office of Women in Development, USAID, Washington DC, 20523
Nomads of the Sahel, Patrick Marnham, Report no. 33, Minority Rights Group, London 1979
The Stories of Vanishing Peoples, John Mercer, Allison & Busby, London 1982
A Closer Look at Deserts, V. Pitt and D. Cook, Hamish Hamilton, 1975
Nature's Landscapes: Deserts and People, James Carson, Wayland, Hove 1982
The Story of Islam, Anthony Kamm, Dinosaur Publications, Cambridge 1976

ACKNOWLEDGEMENTS

Many people have helped with *Two-Way Ticket*. My special thanks to Joy Whitby for inviting me into the series; Doug Wilcox, Alan Harbour and Jane Nairac for all their support and hard work; Jeanne Vickers of UNICEF, Geneva; Annabel McLaren and Carole Ash for their work on the book; Oscar, his family, Dr. Teofilo Altamirano, and World Neighbours in Peru; Marit, her family, Erna L. Haetta, and Hans Ragnar Mathisen in Norway; Latif, his family, and Shireen Huq in Bangladesh; Pauline, her family, David and Lucy Labang in Malaysia; John Gerard, his family, and Coinneach Maclean in the Western Isles; Fatimettou, her family, Tony Raby of UNICEF, and Ahmed Salem ould Vall in Mauritania; and most importantly my own patient and loving family.

Thanks also for permission to reproduce photographs: p.16 (t.r.) Tony & Marion Morrison; (b.l.) Leicester Mercury; p.17 (t.) Coca Cola Bottlers (S & N) Ltd; p.24 (c.r.&l.) Norsk Telegrambyraa Billedarkivet/The Press Association Ltd; (b.r.) Anders Chrs. Cederløv/Nordlys; p.25 (t.r.) Superthorne Panthers Peterborough; p.34 (b.l.), p.35 (t.r., b.c.&r.), p.44 (b.l.) UK UNICEF Nick Fogden; p.35 (b.l.) Tom Learmonth; p.44 (b.r.) Milton Keynes Mirror; p.45 (c.l.) and p.53 (b.c) Rowntree Mackintosh; p.45 (c.r.) and p.53 (t.r.) The National Railway Museum, York; p.53 (c. & b.r.) Leeds United F.C.; pp.16(c.), 17(c.), 34(c.), 35(t.l.), 44(b.c), by the author. Quotations are by kind permission of Merlin Press Ltd., London from Ciro Alegria *Broad and Alien is the World*, 1973; Elle-Han'sa from his poem *Luleju*, 1981; Dr. Basil Greenhill from his book *Boats and Boatmen of Bangladesh*, David & Charles, 1971; Sarawak Museum, East Malaysia from *Sarawak Museum Journal, Special Monograph No. 2, Part II, Poems of Indigenous Peoples of Sarawak, Some of the Songs and Chants*, 1973; Mr. John Lorne Campbell from *Fr. Allan Macdonald of Eriskay*, Oliver & Boyd, 1954; Oxford University Press from H.T. Norris, *Shinqítí Folk Literature and Song*, 1968.

20.-

Arctic Circle

NORWA

Oslo

Eriskay

BRITAIN

London

MAURITANIA • Atar
• Nouakchott

Equator

PERU
Lima •
• Ayacucho